Dear Parents and Educators,

Welcome to Penguin Young Readers! As parents and educators, you know that each child develops at his or her own pace—in terms of speech, critical thinking, and, of course, reading. Penguin Young Readers recognizes this fact. As a result, each Penguin Young Readers book is assigned a traditional easy-to-read level (1–4) as well as a Guided Reading Level (A–P). Both of these systems will help you choose the right book for your child. Please refer to the back of each book for specific leveling information. Penguin Young Readers features esteemed authors and illustrators, stories about favorite characters, fascinating nonfiction, and more!

Do Dolphins Really Smile?

LEVEL **3**

GUIDED READING LEVEL **M**

This book is perfect for a **Transitional Reader** who:
• can read multisyllable and compound words;
• can read words with prefixes and suffixes;
• is able to identify story elements (beginning, middle, end, plot, setting, characters, problem, solution); and
• can understand different points of view.

Here are some **activities** you can do during and after reading this book:
• Research: Do your own research on one of the dolphins listed on pages 16–17. What other facts can you find out?
• Headings: This book is nonfiction, which means it deals with facts that are real. Sometimes as you read, it is hard to understand and remember all the facts. When nonfiction books have headings, it is easier to understand what you read. Headings divide the text into sections. Create headings for this book on sticky papers and place them on the pages. For example, a heading for pages 18–19 could be "Where Do Dolphins Live?"

Remember, sharing the love of reading with a child is the best gift you can give!

—Bonnie Bader, EdM
  Penguin Young Readers program

*Penguin Young Readers are leveled by independent reviewers applying the standards developed by Irene Fountas and Gay Su Pinnell in *Matching Books to Readers: Using Leveled Books in Guided Reading*, Heinemann, 1999.

For Captain Clara and the Dadoba—LD

To those who pursue research to understand
and save the life in the oceans—CW

Penguin Young Readers
Published by the Penguin Group
Penguin Group (USA) Inc., 375 Hudson Street, New York, New York 10014, USA
Penguin Group (Canada), 90 Eglinton Avenue East, Suite 700, Toronto, Ontario M4P 2Y3, Canada
(a division of Pearson Penguin Canada Inc.)
Penguin Books Ltd, 80 Strand, London WC2R 0RL, England
Penguin Ireland, 25 St Stephen's Green, Dublin 2, Ireland (a division of Penguin Books Ltd)
Penguin Group (Australia), 707 Collins Street, Melbourne, Victoria 3008, Australia
(a division of Pearson Australia Group Pty Ltd)
Penguin Books India Pvt Ltd, 11 Community Centre, Panchsheel Park, New Delhi—110 017, India
Penguin Group (NZ), 67 Apollo Drive, Rosedale, Auckland 0632, New Zealand
(a division of Pearson New Zealand Ltd)
Penguin Books, Rosebank Office Park, 181 Jan Smuts Avenue, Parktown North 2193, South Africa
Penguin China, B7 Jaiming Center, 27 East Third Ring Road North,
Chaoyang District, Beijing 100020, China

Penguin Books Ltd, Registered Offices: 80 Strand, London WC2R 0RL, England

Text copyright © 2006 by Laura Driscoll. Illustrations copyright © 2006 by Christina Wald.
All rights reserved. First published in 2006 by Grosset & Dunlap, an imprint of Penguin Group (USA) Inc.
Published in 2013 by Penguin Young Readers, an imprint of Penguin Group (USA) Inc.,
345 Hudson Street, New York, New York 10014. Manufactured in China.

Library of Congress Control Number: 2005027808

ISBN 978-0-448-44341-6   10 9 8 7

Do Dolphins Really Smile?

by Laura Driscoll
illustrated by Christina Wald

Penguin Young Readers
An Imprint of Penguin Group (USA) Inc.

New York Aquarium
Brooklyn, New York
1998

Two dolphins play together in a large pool. Their names are Tab and Presley.

Tab chases Presley. Presley dives down. Tab dives after Presley. Like all dolphins, they love to play!

They like to eat, too. Now it is
feeding time!

A trainer blows a whistle. The
dolphins race to her. She tosses fish
to them. They catch the fish in their
mouths.

Soon feeding time is over. What
is the trainer holding now? Is it
another fish? No. It is a marker. She
makes a mark on Tab's head.

On the other side of the pool,
there is a mirror. Right away Tab
swims to it.

Tab floats in front of the mirror. He looks at himself. He tries to see the mark on his head.

Scientists are watching Tab. Why are they there? They want to know the answer to a question. Does Tab recognize himself? It seems like he does. He looks at the mark.

Tab seems to know it is Tab in the mirror—not some other dolphin.

Besides dolphins, only humans
and apes know their own images
in a mirror.

So dolphins must be very smart. Just *how* smart are they? Scientists don't know for sure. But there is a lot they *do* know about dolphins.

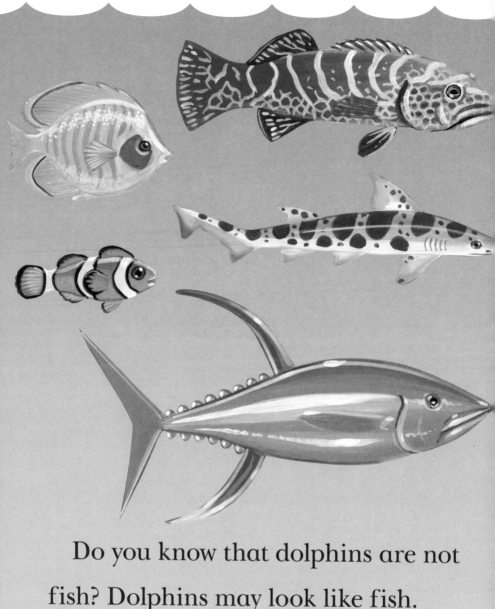

Do you know that dolphins are not fish? Dolphins may look like fish. But fish breathe underwater through slits called gills. Their babies hatch from eggs.

Dolphins are mammals, like dogs
and cows and humans. They breathe
air. They give birth to live babies.
They nurse their young.

Dolphins are a kind of whale. The biggest whales are much bigger than dolphins. But they all belong to the same family.

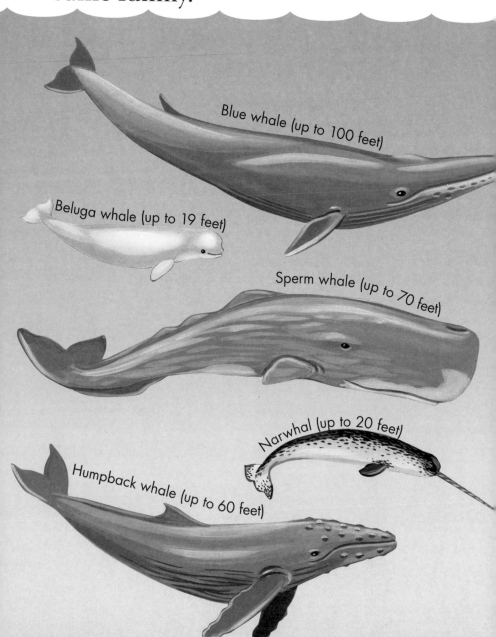

Blue whale (up to 100 feet)

Beluga whale (up to 19 feet)

Sperm whale (up to 70 feet)

Narwhal (up to 20 feet)

Humpback whale (up to 60 feet)

There are many different types of dolphins.

Bottlenose dolphin

Spinner dolphin

Spotted dolphin

Common dolphin

Boto River dolphin

Baiji River dolphin

Dolphins live in many parts of the world.

Some live in the ocean. Some live in rivers.

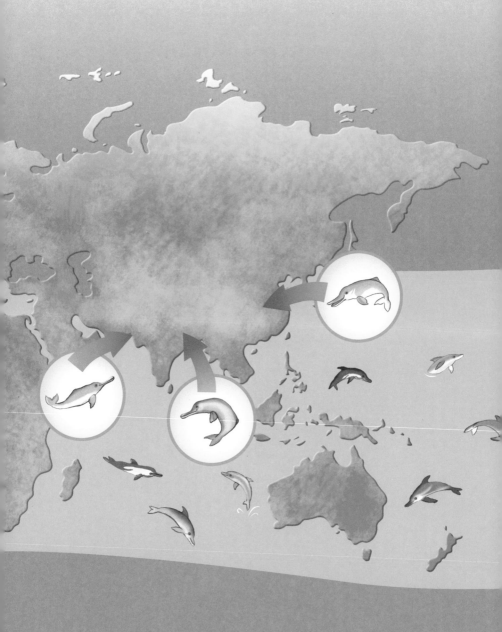

Most dolphins you see in aquariums are bottlenose dolphins. They have sleek bodies and powerful tails. They can swim 30 miles per hour!

These are the dolphins that look like they are smiling. But are they really? Scientists say no. They look this way even when they are scared.

Like all whales, a dolphin must
hold its breath underwater. Some
dolphins can hold their breath for
10 minutes! Then they come up
for air.

There is a hole on top of a dolphin's head. It is called a blowhole.

It opens to take in air. Then the dolphin dives down in the water again.

In the ocean, bottlenose dolphins live in small groups. Sometimes groups will band together. There may be hundreds of dolphins. They swim together. They care for their young together. They hunt for food together.

They form a circle around a group of fish. Some of the dolphins swim into the circle and eat fish. When they are done, the next group of dolphins gets a turn to eat.

How do dolphins work so well together? Some scientists think they "talk" to one another. Lots of animals tell one another things.

Dogs growl to say, "Back off." They whine to show they are scared or hurt.

Their grunts are like happy sighs. And their barks can mean many different things.

Dolphins also make different sounds. They whistle. They squeal. They click—a sound like a creaky door opening.

What do dolphins tell one another?
A scientist did an experiment to
find out. He used one light and two
switches—left and right.

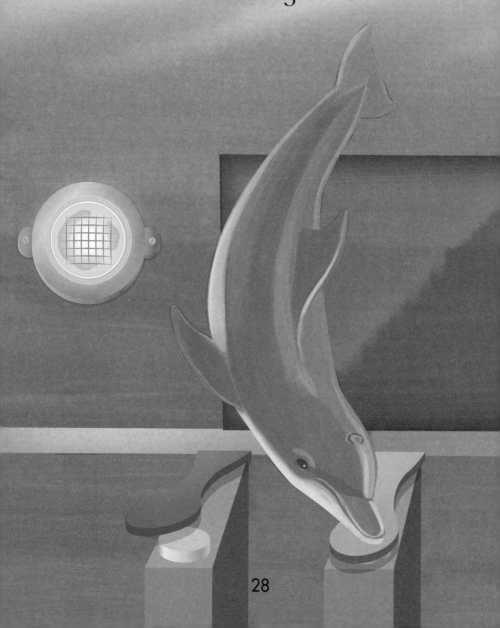

He worked with two dolphins.

Their names were Buzz and Doris.

Sometimes the light came on and stayed on. That told the dolphins to hit the switch on the right. If they both did it, they got a treat—a fish!

Then they were kept apart in the
pool. They could hear each other,
but they could not see each other.
Only Doris could see the light.

The light came on and stayed on. Doris knew to hit the right switch. But Buzz did not know because he could not see the light. Doris wanted her fish! And they *both* had to hit the right switch for her to get it. She made a sound.

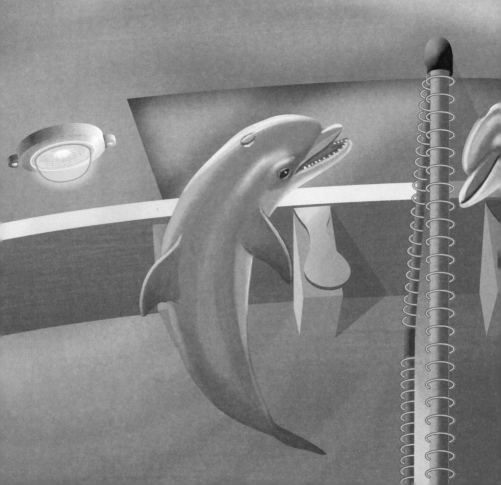

Buzz heard it. Then he hit the right switch! They both got their fish. The scientist did the test over and over. Buzz knew the switch to hit almost every time. How did he know? Did Doris tell him?

This dolphin looks for food in a coral reef. She has a sponge on her snout. Why did she put it there? Because the coral is sharp. She may be using the sponge to protect her snout.

It is a smart thing for a dolphin to do. Very smart.

These are the dolphin's babies.
They also put sponges on their
snouts.

Did the mama dolphin teach them to? Some scientists think so.

So dolphins may be good teachers.
They are definitely good students!
Dolphins in tanks learn lots of tricks.
And they learn them quickly.

They stand
on their tails
and dance on
the water.

They do flips
in the air.

They wave hello with their flippers.

At one aquarium, bits of trash sometimes got in the pool. Eating trash can make dolphins very sick.

So the trainers had an idea. They trained the dolphins to help clean the pool.

Each time the dolphins brought trash, they got some fish. The dolphins seemed to like this new game.

One dolphin
came back again,
and again, and
again.

Each time, he had
more trash.

Each time, he
got more fish.

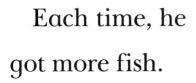

But one thing didn't make sense. The pool looked clean. So where was the dolphin finding all the trash?

The dolphin had a secret stash of trash! He had found lots of trash. He had stuffed it all in a bag in one corner of the pool.

Why did he do this? To get fish!

When he wanted a snack, he swam to the hidden trash.

He picked out a tiny piece, or he tore off a small bit. He wanted his stash to last.

Then he took the trash to the
trainer . . . and got his fish!

The dolphin's new trick was to
trick the trainers!

So maybe dolphins don't smile. But that one sure got the last laugh!